# I want to be a Vet

Other titles in this series:

I want to be a Cowboy
I want to be a Doctor
I want to be a Firefighter
I want to be a Pilot
I want to be a Police Officer

# I WANT TO BE A

# Vet

**DAN LIEBMAN**

## FIREFLY BOOKS

# A Firefly Book

Published by Firefly Books Ltd. 2000

Fourth printing, 2004

**Library of Congress Cataloging-in-Publication Data is available**

**National Library of Canada Cataloging-in-Publication Data**

Liebman, Daniel
    I want to be a vet

ISBN 1-55209-471-5 (bound)   ISBN 1-55209-469-3 (pbk.)

1. Veterinarians – Juvenile literature.   I. Title

SF756.L53 2000                j636.089'06952        C99-932466-7

Published in Canada in 2000 by
Firefly Books Ltd.
66 Leek Crescent
Richmond Hill, Ontario
L4B 1H1

Published in the United States in 2000 by
Firefly Books (U.S.) Inc.
P.O. Box 1338, Ellicott Station
Buffalo, New York, USA
14205

**Photo Credits**

© First Light/John Curtis, front cover.
© Werner Bokelberg, The Image Bank, page 5.
© Patti McConville, The Image Bank, page 6.
© John Howard; Cordaiy Photo Library Ltd./ CORBIS, page 7.
© John Periam; Cordaiy Photo Library Ltd./ CORBIS, page 8.
© Kit Houghton Photography/CORBIS, page 9.
© Philip Gould/CORBIS, pages 10 & 11.
© Michael Salas, The Image Bank, pages 12-13.

© Tim Wright/CORBIS, page 14.
© Raymond Gehman/ CORBIS, page 15.
© Lynda Richardson/CORBIS, page 16.
© Steve Kaufman/CORBIS, page 17.
© Dan Guravich/CORBIS, page 18.
© Richard T. Nowitz/CORBIS, page 19.
© Lowell Georgia/CORBIS, pages 20-21.
© First Light/Stephen Homer, page 22.
© Wolfgang Kaehler/CORBIS, page 23.
© Layne Kennedy/CORBIS, page 24.

Design by Interrobang Graphic Design Inc.
Printed and bound in Canada by Friesens, Altona, Manitoba

*The Publisher acknowledges the financial support of the Government of Canada through the Book Publishing Industry Development Program for its publishing activities.*

Animals need doctors, just as people do. A doctor who treats animals is called a vet, which is short for veterinarian.

Vets work with all kinds of animals. This dog is having a paw examined during its yearly checkup.

This nurse holds the cat still while the vet clips the cat's nails.

Like children, dogs need shots to help them grow up strong and healthy. This pup is about to get its first shot.

Horses, too, need a vet's help. This vet checks the animal's teeth while the owner holds the rope.

Sometimes cows are placed in a special stall to keep them from hurting themselves and the vet.

This newborn calf needs to be dried and warmed right away. She is only a few minutes old, but already weighs more than you do!

This large horse is having an operation. The vet has given the horse a shot to make sure it won't feel any pain. Like people, most animals recover quickly and are ready to go home in a few days.

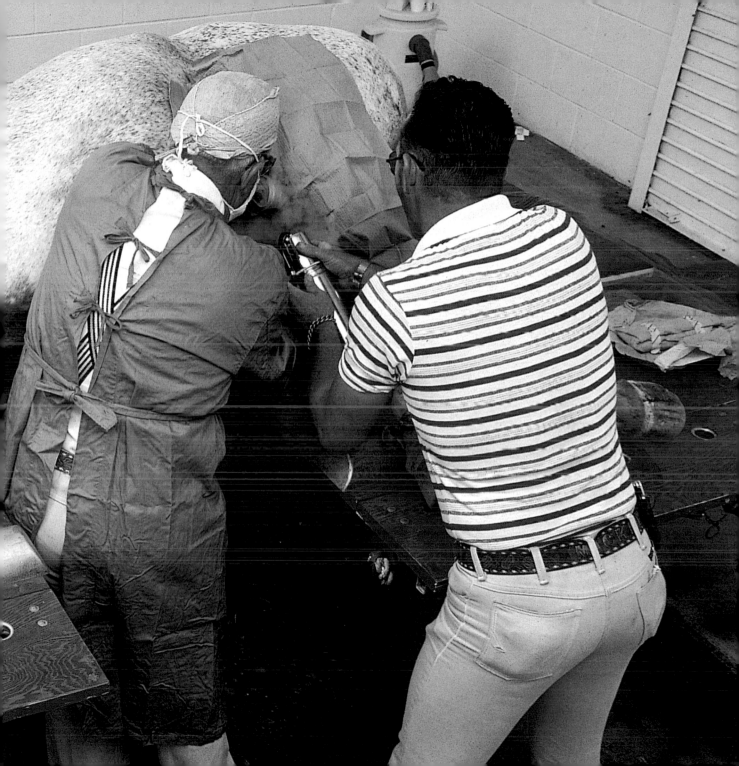

Country vets spend most of their time working at farms. These piglets have just been born.

This girl wants her pet lamb to know that everything will be fine.

Animals like this bear cub need special care when their mothers aren't around to look after them.

Vets know how to take care of animals caught in the wild.

The vet and his assistants are operating on this injured bald eagle.

This vet is checking the dolphin's breathing. Because dolphins are so clever, they often do just what the vet wants them to do.

Looking after whales can be dangerous work. The vet and his team must be very careful when handling such a large animal.

Vets at zoos take care of animals from all over the world, like this wallaby from Australia.

It is much harder to give medicine to a llama than to a dog or a cat!

Vets can't ask the patient what the problem is. This vet is testing the little owl's vision.